What's My Family Tree?

**Mick Manning
and Brita Granström**

FRANKLIN WATTS
LONDON·SYDNEY

**For Max with love
from Mum and Dad**

First published in 2001
by Franklin Watts,
96 Leonard Street,
London EC2A 4XD

Franklin Watts Australia
56 O'Riordan Street
Alexandria NSW 2015

Text and illustrations © 2001
Mick Manning and Brita Granström

Editor: Rachel Cooke
Art director: Jonathan Hair

Printed in Hong Kong
A CIP catalogue record is available
from the British Library.
Dewey Classification 306.8
ISBN 0 7496 3997 0

Contents

What's my family tree?   5

Why is it called a family tree?   7

And where do I fit in?   7

What about Mum and Dad?   8

Do we all have a mum and dad?   9

Why did Mum and Dad want a baby?   10

Why do I look like I do?   11

Why am I good at things Mum and Dad can't do?   12

So what's a family then?   14

Are there other sorts of families?   16

What are one-parent families?   18

And why don't some children live with their real parents? 19

What about other relatives – cousins and things?   20

So what are my grans and grandads?   23

Why have I only one grandad?   23

So who were my great-grandparents?   24

It's like a history story!   24

Will my family tree keep growing?   26

Yours is only one tree in a whole forest!   28

A family tree   30

Useful word index   32

What's my family tree?

Your family tree is a sort of 'family map', stretching back through the centuries.
It shows all your family and how you are related to them.
We all have our own family tree, but it is not often written down.

Why is it called a family tree?

Because families join together when people have children or get married, so the map grows a new part or branch – it starts to look a bit like a tree . . .

And where do I fit in?

You're a new name on the family map – a sort of new shoot on your family tree. You are joined to a branch that's your mum and dad!

Mum

Dad

Ask Mum or Dad to show you pictures of when they were young.

What about Mum and Dad?

Your mum and dad were babies once, too! They both came from different families, each with its own family tree.

One day they met each other and became friends. Perhaps they lived together, or got married. Then, after a while, they had a baby and that was the beginning of your family branch!

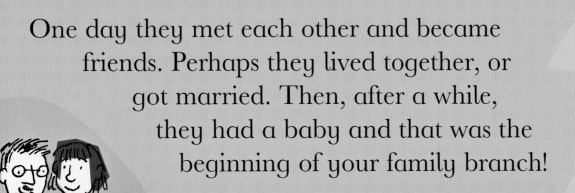

Do we all have a mum and dad?

Yes, we all need to have a dad when we are made – and we need a mum to grow inside! They are Mum and Dad – our birth parents.

Sometimes, children don't stay with their birth parents but are adopted. Their adopted parents become Mum and Dad instead.

Why did Mum and Dad want a baby?

Well that's difficult to answer! But most people have a baby because they love each other very much and know that their baby will be a mixture of them both.

Why do I look like I do?

You are unique – there has never been anyone like you before in the world! But you inherit qualities from your parents, from the way you look to the way you think.

Mum

Dad

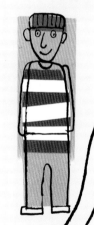

brown eyes
blond hair
fast runner
curly hair

blue eyes
short legs
brown hair
sharp eyes
straight hair

Me

You may look like your mum or your dad – or a mixture of both.

Sometimes you inherit your looks from people further back in your family tree.

Why am I good at things Mum and Dad can't do?

Well, maybe it's just natural talent – part of being uniquely you! Or maybe you get it from one 'side' of the family? Just like your looks, you can inherit talents from grandparents or ancestors from long ago!

Great-great-great-great-grandpa Ravi

Great-great-aunty Vita

So when you suddenly show a talent for football or painting, sometimes your family can't think where it comes from!

Great-grandpa Stanley

Great-great-granny Dora

Do you take after someone in particular?

Great-great-auntie Ingrid

Great-great-great-uncle Albert

So what's a family then?

A family usually means Mum and Dad and their children – you and any brothers and sisters (your siblings) you may have. They are your 'close' family.

Brothers and sisters are children
who have the same parents as you.
Half-brothers or half-sisters are
siblings that share one parent with
you — that's when Mum or Dad has
had a baby with someone else.

There is no such thing as a 'normal' family. A family can be all sorts of different mixtures: Dad and his friend; Mum and her partner; Auntie Sue and Cousin Jack; maybe your gran or grandad look after you a lot.

It doesn't matter what your close family is like, just so long as you all love and look after each other.

What are one-parent families?

Sometimes mums and dads split up. They don't want to live together any more and one of them moves out. Children often then get two homes – one to live in and one to visit in the holidays.

Sadly, too, sometimes either Mum or Dad dies. The other parent is left on their own with the children.

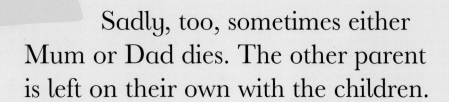

And why don't some children live with their real parents?

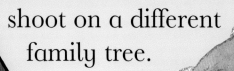

Sometimes parents can't look after their children, even though they may want to. Then the children can be looked after by foster parents for a while. But sometimes these children are adopted by other parents forever – and become a new shoot on a different family tree.

What about other relatives – cousins and things?

Your relatives are all the people on your family tree. If your mum and dad have any brothers or sisters, they are your uncles and aunts. If your uncles and aunts have any children, they are your cousins!

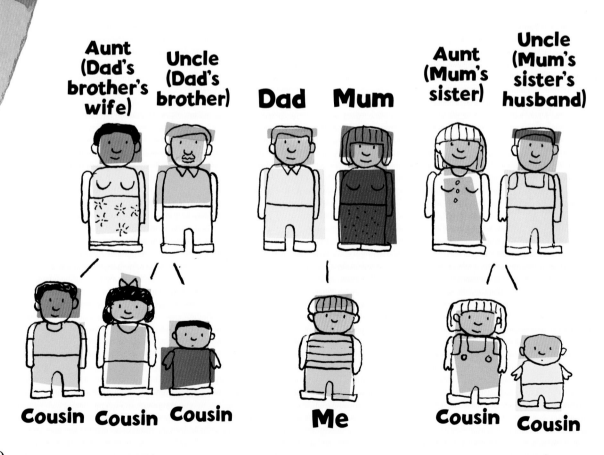

Aunt (Dad's brother's wife) Uncle (Dad's brother) Dad Mum Aunt (Mum's sister) Uncle (Mum's sister's husband)

Cousin Cousin Cousin Me Cousin Cousin

Relatives like this are some of the nearest
of the other branches on your family tree.
They may live nearby – or in a far-away country!

So what are my grans and grandads?

Grans and grandads are our mum's mum and dad, and our dad's mum and dad. You have four of them on your family tree.

Why have I only one grandad?

Some grans and grandads may be dead – but they are remembered on your family tree.

Ask to see some photos of them . . .

23

So who were my great-grandparents?

Your great-grandparents were your gran's and grandad's mums and dads, so you've got eight of them! They were born a long time ago.

It's like a history story!

Try saying 'great-grandad' then add some more greats at the beginning . . . Each great goes back about 25 years – the more greats you add, the further back in history you go!

Granny & Grandad

Great-great-great-great-granny & grandad

Great-great-great-great-great-great-granny & grandad

great-
great-
great-
great-
great-great-
great-great-
great...

Great x 16 granny & grandad

Great x 26 granny & grandad

Great x 46 granny & grandad

You can usually trace your family tree back about 200 years. After that, just imagine who your relatives might have been!

Great x 500 granny & grandad

25

Will my family tree keep growing?

Yes! It's growing all the time. Your mum and dad may have more children. And perhaps when you grow up, you will have a baby. But right now you're the fresh, new shoot, on the brand new branch, on your very, very old family tree . . .

And remember this . . .

Yours is only one tree in a whole forest!

A family tree

Great-grandparents

Great-grandparents

Great-aunt   Great-uncle

Gran and Grandad

Great-uncle   Great-aunt
and lots of children I can't fit in!

Uncle   Aunt

Uncle's ex

Uncle

Aunt

Aunt's ex

Mum

Cousin   Cousin

Cousin   Cousin

These cousins are stepbrothers and stepsister

Stepcousin

Brother

A family tree looks like this. Why not draw your own and see how many branches you can fill in?

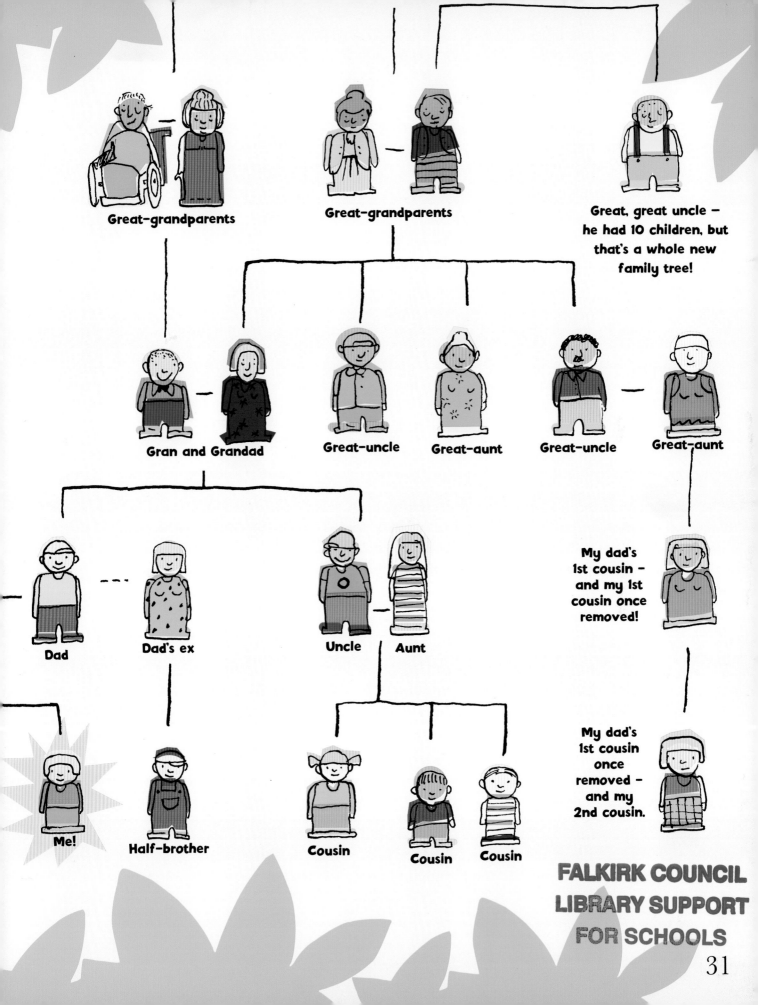

Great-grandparents

Great-grandparents

Great, great uncle – he had 10 children, but that's a whole new family tree!

Gran and Grandad

Great-uncle

Great-aunt

Great-uncle

Great-aunt

Dad

Dad's ex

Uncle

Aunt

My dad's 1st cousin – and my 1st cousin once removed!

Me!

Half-brother

Cousin

Cousin

Cousin

My dad's 1st cousin once removed – and my 2nd cousin.

Useful word index

adopted We are adopted children if our parents have become our mum and dad by law, but they are not our parents by birth. Pages 9, 19

ancestors People who were born before us to whom we are related. Page 12

aunt The sister of our mother or father. Pages 17, 20, 30, 31

birth parents A woman and man who have a baby together. Page 9

brother A boy who has the same parents as us. Pages 4, 15, 20, 30

cousin The children of our aunts and uncles. They are our first cousins. Our second cousins are the children of our parent's first cousins. Pages 17, 20, 30, 31

family tree A kind of map or plan that shows all our relatives and how they are related to us. Pages 5, 7, 8, 11, 19, 20, 21, 23, 25, 27, 30-31

foster parents People who, for a short time, will act as children's parents because their real parents can not do so. Page 19

grandparents The parents of our mum and dad. Pages 12, 17, 23, 25, 30, 31

great- The word we add before a relative such as aunt or grandparent to show they are from further back

in our family tree. Each great we add takes us one step back. Pages 13, 24, 25, 30, 31

half-brother A brother who either our mum or dad has had with another partner. Pages 15, 30

half-sister A sister who either our mum or dad has had with another partner. Page 15

inherit To be born with something, such as our looks or a talent, that has been passed through our family. Pages 11, 12

one-parent families Families where only one parent (either a mum or dad) is looking after the children. Page 18

parents Our mum and dad. Mums and dads get a mention on nearly every page of this book!

relatives All the people in a family. Pages 20, 21, 25

siblings Our brothers and sisters. Page 14

sister A girl who has the same parents as us. Pages 14, 15, 20

step- The word we add before a relative, such as brother or mother, to show that we are related by marriage but not by birth. Page 30

uncle The brother of our mother or father. Pages 20, 30, 31